How Your Local Government Works

A Guide for Residents of Yorubaland

By Adeyinka Shoyemi

How Your Local Government Works
A Guide for Residents of Yorubaland
A guide to how local governments work for anyone currently involved in or interested in getting involved in local community activity.

First Published in 2012
Economic Initiative, London
adeyinka.shoyemi@yahoo.co.uk

Contents

A Guide for Residents of Yorubaland

Introduction

The Economic Initiative has published this guide as part of a more comprehensive programme of activities to support and strengthen community empowerment and engagement.

The Economic Initiative influences regional urban policy to bring about effective change for local communities by acting as a bridge between policymakers and the community sector.

The Economic Initiative undertakes research and policy development, produces information and organises activities, all designed to inform policy development and help community groups influence decision-making.

In all our work, we bring together people from various backgrounds to develop ideas that will shape the debate in Yorubaland and beyond and engage a broad and diverse audience worldwide.

Local Government Areas and Local Council Development Areas

ocal government affects everybody's life. Councils are responsible for delivering essential services in local areas and dealing with local matters and issues. They are also the cornerstone of democracy, allowing local people to directly shape local services and issues by electing local councillors and chairpersons.

This guide for local governments is for anyone who participates or wants to participate in local community activities. It sets out

The different types of local governments in Yorubaland.

The role of elected chairpersons and councillors.

How local governments work with other parts of the public sector.

Tips on getting to know your local government and getting in touch.

Where to get more information.

DID YOU KNOW?

There are 159 local government areas in Yorubaland.

There are over 159 local council development areas.

There are over 2,000 elected local councillors in Yorubaland.

Local government employs over 120,000 people working in around 300 different functions.

There are around 2,000 wards. Local governments spend over ₦60 billion a year.

Overview

---

he government has determined to increase local people's
involvement and levels of responsibility in shaping the services
they receive. All the main political parties agree that creating
more opportunities for people to influence local decisions and service
delivery is essential. This comes when there are concerns about how
many people must turn away from local politics as voters and potential
elected councillors or chairpersons.

This is important because local governments, led by democratically
elected chairmen and local councillors, provide many services that
make communities work. And while they don't offer all the services
directly, they are typically involved as active partners with others who
do.

Local government is the closest level to the population and, thus, the
most important facilitator of economic and social development at the
local level.

The scale and reach of local government, the complexity and degree of change taking place, and the extent to which individuals, communities, and organisations are encouraged to get involved make it vital that everyone understands it better.

The scale and reach of local government... makes it vital that everyone understands it better.

Types of Local Governments in Yorubaland

ocal government in Yorubaland exists in a single-tier, all-purpose council responsible for all local authority services and functions. These are called local government areas and local council development areas.

There are 159 local government areas and more than 200 local council development areas in Yorubaland. Table 1 shows the distribution of these councils across Yorubaland:

Structure of Local Government in Yorubaland.

State	Lagos	Ogun	Oyo	Osun	Ondo	Ekiti	Kwara	Kogi	Delta	Edo
LGA	20	20	33	30	18	16	12	6	3	1
LCDA	37	37	35	31	–	19	–	–	–	–
Ward	245	236	351	332	203	177	193	72	36	12

LGA: Local Government Areas
LCDA: Local Council Development Areas

Note: Kwara State has 16 local government areas in which 12 are Yoruba-speaking councils; Kogi State has 21 local government areas in which only 6 are Yoruba-speaking councils; Delta State has 25 local government areas in which 3 are Yoruba-Itsekiri councils; and Edo State has 18 local government areas in which 1 is Yoruba-speaking local council. Only the Yoruba-speaking local councils and wards have been recognised and listed in the above table.

How Local Elections Work

ocal people elect all local government chairpersons and councillors for a three-year term. Local elections usually occur every three years; council elections are generally held in Yorubaland yearly.

Local government councils are divided into wards. Each ward elects a single member to the council. The system is consistent across Yorubaland. Decision-making within each council is done through a system of committees; however, there is a division between the executive and the legislative bodies. Councils range in size from 10 to 15 councillors in each local government.

Local council development areas are semi-autonomous areas divided into wards, where a councillor represents each ward. Elections take place every three years in all councils for all seats.

According to Nigeria's unitary system of government, local government is created through state legislation with the approval of the National Assembly. The states are political bodies, with elections to their legislatures taking place every four years. Each State has a Commissioner responsible for local government. Their role is to develop policy and legislation relating to local government and to provide oversight.

In several states, elected councillors and the chairpersons of local government authorities have been suspended by the state governor or state assemblies with the due process of law by not allowing the chairpersons and councillors to exercise their role. In this case, the governors appointed transition committees to replace them.

All councillors and chairpersons stand for election on behalf of the main political parties in Yorubaland. There are no "independent" candidates standing for election.

After every election, the political party that wins the chairmanship seat takes control of the local government. As the council leader, the elected chairperson will allocate councillors to critical positions within the council.

Elected Councillors, Roles and Responsibilities

lected chairpersons and councillors are responsible for making decisions on behalf of their local community about local services such as preschool, primary and adult education; public health (including primary care and health protection); town and regional planning; roads and transport; refuse collection; cemeteries and crematoria; environmental protection; sports; leisure services; and religious facilities.

They agree on the council's budget, set the policy framework, appoint committees and make constitutional decisions. They also represent those people living and working in their wards and act as advocates on their behalf while at the same time helping to provide leadership for the area as a whole.

Under the unitary system, local government is created by state legislation with the endorsement of the National Assembly. The states are political bodies, with elections to their legislatures taking place every four years. Each state has a commissioner who is responsible for local government.

How the Local Government Structure Works

---

he decision-making within each local government is done through a committee system. All councillors and chairpersons come together at full council meetings. These meetings consider high-level budgetary and political decisions and examine other essential matters. However, there is a division between the executive and the legislature.

The Executive:

Legislation gives local government authorities powers to establish executive committees separate from its monitoring (scrutiny) functions. Authorities have the discretion to establish other committees ad hoc by state legislation. Chairpersons are directly elected and serve full-time, and are remunerated accordingly. The executive committees are constituted by the chairperson, with responsibilities determined by state government legislation. There is little difference between the 174 Local Government Areas and the 37 Local Council Development Areas.

The Cabinet (or directly elected executive):

The cabinet is the local government's main decision-making body. It is headed by the chairperson and made up of elected councillors responsible for particular aspects of the local government's priorities. These portfolio holders often carry cross-cutting responsibilities (town planning, environment, or children's services). Together, these portfolio holders recommend a budget for each year, which needs approval from the full council.

Find out who your local councillor is and which Cabinet member is responsible for issues that interest you or your community groups.

Once that has happened, the cabinet is generally left to make the necessary decisions to deliver local government services – acting within the budget and the already agreed-on local government-wide policies.

The cabinet usually reflects the political balance of the local government as a whole. Where the local government comprises councillors from mostly one party, the whole cabinet will reflect this.

Meetings of the executive committee and the cabinet are generally open to the public to attend and, with notice, make short contributions. The cabinet can exclude the public from some meetings where business items are confidential or relate to particular individuals.

Overview and Scrutiny:

Each State has an auditor general to whom local authorities must submit their annual accounts to scrutinise and oversee decisions taken by the cabinet. The main functions of scrutiny are:

(i) To hold the Cabinet accountable by examining their proposals and decisions:

Evaluating policies, performance and progress.

Ensuring that consultation, where necessary, has been carried out.

Highlighting areas for improvement.

(ii) To ensure high-quality services meet the community's needs by reviewing services:

Developing policies to make services better.

Ensuring that people are consulted when changes are proposed.

Ensuring that services represent value for money.

(iii) To consult the public on the services it wants by:

Ensuring the local government knows what communities care about.

Making sure they know about the scrutiny process and how to get involved.

Local Government Officers, Roles and Responsibilities

---

hile councillors, with the chairperson, set the direction of the local government and create the policy framework for service delivery, local authority officers, led by the director of administration, advise the local government and are responsible for effective service delivery. Each local authority directly appoints the Director of Administration and junior staff, while the Local Government Services Commission hires senior managers.

The experience that officers gain over time about how local government works, legislation and the particular council and its communities is essential in helping councillors and chairpersons do their jobs. This may mean that there are times when they have to tell councillors and the chairperson that they cannot carry out a course of action they are saying they want to. Officers must provide professional, non-partisan advice.

Local government workers include teachers, public servants, and others.

All local governments will have leaflets explaining how decisions are made. Visit your local government office to see the information available, or visit their website.

Legal Responsibilities and Powers of Local Government

Local government generally plans and delivers the most strategic services, such as education, child welfare, transportation, road services, tax collection, regional planning, permits and waste collection.

Summary of the services of the different types of authority:

Service	Delivering Authority		
	FG	SG	LGA
Pre-School			*
Kindergarten and Nursery			*
Primary School		*	*
Secondary School	*	*	
Higher Education	*	*	
Adult Education			*
Primary Healthcare			*
Hospitals	*	*	
Health Protection			*
Town and Regional Planning		*	*
Transport Planning	*	*	*
Passenger Transport	*		
Rail/Ports/Airport	*		
Fire	*	*	
Libraries	*	*	
Leisure and Recreation	*	*	*
Parks and Open Space			*
Waster Collection and Disposal			*
Environmental Protection		*	*
Police	*		

Budget

ocal governments collect some local taxes, such as haulage, markets, and motor and commercial drivers' levies, which raise about 1% of revenue. The remainder of the budget comes from the federal government's statutory allocation and fees for local services. Federal and state governments set business rates or local licences, fees and fines, contributing about 17% of regional revenue.

Local governments raise their income in various ways. Taxes, rents, permits, fees, and fines account for approximately 30% of revenues.

Relationships with Other Parts of the Public Sector

he federal government is responsible for policing, whereas it shares responsibility for fire and civil defence provisions across the country with state governments.

The provision of health services is generally carried out by the Federal and State Governments, except for a few services made exclusive to the federal government through the Federal Ministry of Health. State governments are responsible for secondary hospital care and support local governments in providing primary health care – state planning, operational support, coordination, monitoring, and training.

Community Leadership

s elected bodies and providers of many services to local people, local governments have a vital role in leading their communities. Elected local governments are constitutionally entrenched and must

Promote the community's economic, social and environmental well-being.

Collection of taxes and fees.

Establishment and maintenance of cemeteries, burial grounds and homes for the needy or infirm.

Licensing of bicycles and trucks (other than mechanically propelled trucks).

Establishment, maintenance and regulation of markets, motor parks and public conveniences.

Construction and maintenance of roads, streets, drains and other public highways, parks, and open spaces.

Naming of roads and streets and numbering of houses.

Provision and maintenance of public transportation and refuse disposal.

Registration of births, deaths and marriages.

Assessment of privately owned houses or tenements to levy such rates as may be prescribed by the House of Assembly of a State.

Control and regulation of outdoor advertising, movement and keeping of pets of all descriptions, shops and kiosks, restaurants and other places to sell food to the public, and laundries.

Invite your local Councillor to Community Group meetings or any activities you have planned. He may be pleased to give a brief speech about the council. The counsellor may be too busy to attend, but the invitation will raise awareness about your group and the issues you are interested in.

There are also several specific legal roles that local governments are playing with state governments on issues such as:

The provision and maintenance of primary education.

The development of agriculture and natural resources, other than the exploitation of minerals.

The provision and maintenance of health services.

The chairperson and councillors are elected representatives of their communities. The chairperson is typically elected but can also be appointed under exceptional circumstances. They supervise the activities of the local government and preside over all council meetings.

Focusing on specific issues, committees play a vital role in the council's day-to-day business. They assist the Council in making decisions and are generally required to report their discussions to the Council.

A local government council is central to socio-economic planning and development in its authority area. Being the level of government closest to the people, it is considered the most important facilitator of economic and social development at the grassroots level.

Holding Local Government to Account

---

ach year, the state government reviews the efficiency of each local government and the quality of all its services. Carried out by the office of the auditor general for Local Governments, the state looks across the whole range of local government services and considers how well they have done overall.

The Office of the Auditor General of Local Governments will continue to audit the accounts of the local governments in Yorubaland and their agencies. It will examine the performance of specific indicators and the full range of services provided to meet them.

The Office focuses on:

An area assessment of how well local public services, such as community safety, health, and environmental services, deliver better results for local people and how likely they will improve.

Organisational assessments for each local government agency will assess their performance and use of resources.

Many councillors have offices where people can go for advice and information. Suppose you are an individual, a new community group, or have recently joined one. In that case, you can use this to introduce yourself and your group and raise any issues.

The Office of the Auditor General of local governments also focuses on what is achieved by local authorities working alone and collaborating with others to achieve their goals. The Auditor General's assessments and judgements are broadly based on the annual accounts of local authorities to review and monitor decisions made by the Cabinet.

Greater emphasis is placed on what local people think of the services provided to them by the local authorities and on how open and comprehensible the process is to the public.

Community Engagement

he government wants to ensure local authorities give people more opportunities to actively participate in shaping local services.

All local governments already provide various ways for local people to get involved in specific areas, such as town and regional planning.

The government wants more local involvement in its communities to rapidly increase productivity and service delivery capacity, which will significantly expand the role of local councils.

The government wants local governments to engage their communities in three significant ways:

(i) Providing information.
(ii) Consulting.
(iii) Involvement in decision-making.

Local government authorities must ensure they involve representatives of local persons in any activities relating to changing, improving or otherwise making things different. Representing local people means people who live, work, study, play or visit the area. Examples of what might come under these involvements include:

Many local governments have leaflets and online information about opportunities to get involved and have your say. Find out what is going on and get involved!

Influencing decisions. Providing feedback on decisions, services, and policies, working with the local government authority to develop new policies and services, carrying out some particular services for the authority, and working with the local authority to assess services.

The involvement of the local people is a vital part of meeting the expectations of the government and the people of Yorubaland by building an efficient, effective and proactive professional council. It will make it easier for citizens and communities to hold local government councils and other public agencies accountable for their decisions and performance.

In a democracy, power belongs to the people, and all public officials have their positions in trust. The local council is always obliged to uphold transparency and accountability.

How to Contact Your Local Government

nyone may contact their local government about local services. You can talk to an elected official about your issues. When your immediate contact cannot help you, or you need to speak to another person or department, they will generally redirect you. Sometimes, when you want to comment on a planning plan that affects you, you can be asked to give a specific response, often in writing.

Using this guide to How Your Local Government Works, you should see where best to make your enquiry (local government offices or elected councillor) and whether you need to speak to someone in the local or state government.

See overleaf for more details.

Contacts and Top Tips

The main ways to make contact with your local government council.

In-person:
You can visit the main local government offices and speak to someone face to face.

Online:
You can directly access a wide range of local governments online. You can do this through the internet address of your local government if you know it.

By Phone:
You can call the local government's main telephone number.

By Letter:
You can write to the local government council's offices. You can also
find contact details online or through local information points such as
libraries.

www.lagosstate.gov.ng
www.oyostate.gov.ng
www.ogunstate.gov.ng
www.osunstate.gov.ng
www.ekitistate.gov.ng
www.ondostate.gov.ng
www.kwarastate.gov.ng
www.kogistatenigeria.org
www.edostate.gov.ng
www.deltastate.gov.ng

Top tips for getting involved or learning more about your local government area.

Ensure you know which local government or council development area covers the area you live or work in or where your community group is active.

Find out who your local councillor is and who on the committee is responsible for issues of interest to you or your community groups.

All local governments will have leaflets explaining how decisions are taken, how people can stay informed, and what opportunities the public can attend meetings, ask questions, and submit petitions. Visit your local government to see their available information, or look online.

Many councillors have offices where people can go for advice and information. Find out where they are. If you are a new community group or have recently joined one, you may use this opportunity to introduce yourself and your group and raise any issues.

Find out when the next election round is and ensure you are registered to vote.

Many local governments have leaflets and online information about opportunities to get involved and have your say. Find out what is going on and get involved!

www.ingramcontent.com/pod-product-compliance
Lightning Source LLC
Chambersburg PA
CBHW071003250726
48663CB00002B/364